GW00361430

John Earley

Bird Keeping

for the young and young-at-heart

Illustrated by
Gordon Parkinson

Contents

BIRD KEEPING

Foreword

The advice and antics of John Earley's cartoon character 'Chirpy' in the monthly magazine *Bird keeper* have kept its readers informed and entertained over the years. Chirpy's tips are popular with the young and not-so-young, the beginner bird keeper and even the more experienced hobbyist – in fact, anyone who wants essential birdcare facts presented in a highly readable form with a chuckle thrown in for good measure.

It is pleasing therefore to see that John Earley has continued with the 'Chirpy formula' in this offering for the younger bird keeper. It is packed with tips and hints to help the young beginner avoid the common pitfalls which await the unwary hobbyist.

In addition to all the sound advice, there is plenty of useful information (joining a bird club, glossary of bird-keeping terms and so on) to introduce the uninitiated to a fascinating pastime.

The snappy, cheery format of *Bird Keeping* will, I suspect, also attract the eye of a few 'old hands'. But in our hobby, there is never a time when we 'know it all'.

Peter Moss
Editor-in-Chief
Cage & Aviary Birds and *Bird keeper*

Chapter 1

Bird biography

Congratulations on wanting to keep birds and buying this book.
You are about to join one of the oldest and friendliest of
hobbies, bird keeping.

Which bird are you going to buy? A Foreign Finch,
canary or budgerigar? They are all equally suitable
and have a basic diet of easy-to-get seed. This
book will help you to make your choice. So read on!

> **Did you know?**
> *The first mention of bird keeping is
> in the 14th century book,* Historia
> Animalium.

Bird keeping through the ages

By 3000 BC man had already started to use birds of prey to help in the hunt for food.
Birds were domesticated during the second century BC. The
British Museum has an ancient work of art depicting life in the
year 400 BC. It shows a schoolboy with a
pet quail.

> **Did you know?**
> *The quail is a small, plumpish,
> ground-dwelling bird.*

The first bird to live
and breed in a cage
was the canary. The
Germans seem to have been
breeding and exporting the canary in the 16th century.
Birdcage Walk in London got its name from the 'road of
aviaries' created by Charles II in the 17th century. It is on
the south side of St James Park, near Buckingham Palace.

Before this, many ordinary men and women who lived near
seaports had seen exotic birds. It was not uncommon to see
a sailor returning from
afar with a talking parrot on his shoulder.
By the eighteenth century, rich people
were keeping birds in properly-
planned ornamental aviaries.

> **Did you know?**
> *The* Historia Animalium *calls the canary 'the
> bird with the sweetest song'.*
> *Charles II reigned from 1660 to 1685. So
> Birdcage Walk is over 300 years old.*

Meanwhile the working man was
using the canary for safety. Coal miners
always took a canary down the mine.
When it stopped singing, this was a warning that
deadly gases were present. The last canaries were 'retired' in 1996.

Bird keeping became really popular in the second half of the 19th century. John Gould, a naturalist, brought the budgerigar (or budgie) back to the United Kingdom on his return from Australia in 1840. It was originally known as the lovebird because of the way a pair sits closely together. The bird now known as the Lovebird comes from Africa.

> **Did you know?**
> *The budgerigar is a member of the parrot family and is found in the wild only in Australia.*

It didn't take much longer for the budgie to reach the United States where it is known by the name parakeet. By then it was well on its way to becoming the universally popular creature it is today.

What is a bird?

> **Did you know?**
> *Fossils of Archaeopteryx have been found in Bavaria, Germany.*
> *The Hoatzin's home is in the Amazon Basin in South America.*

Birds are probably descended from the Archaeopteryx which died out about 150 million years ago. The size of a pigeon, it was similar to a reptile in some ways. It had a long tail, was covered in feathers and may have been warm blooded.

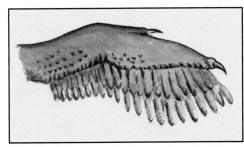

Archaeopteryx also had teeth and 'grasping hands' at the front of its wings. Some birds, such as the Hoatzin, still have a claw at the front of the wing. The Hoatzin is probably the strangest bird alive today. It is also the closest living relative of the Archaeopteryx still in existence.

The Hoatzin's face looks as though it is made up from bits unwanted by other birds. As a chick it has two 'climbing claws' on each wing, and can swim but not fly. As an adult, it flies but cannot swim and has lost its claws.

> **Did you know?**
> *No one can agree whether the Hoatzin is a member of the pheasant or cuckoo family.*

Birds belong to the class of the animal kingdom called *Aves*. They are all warm-blooded, covered with feathers, lay eggs and have a skeleton. Some species are more colourful than others and the female (hen) is normally duller than the male (cock).

AM I TOO OLD FOR A SWIM?

Why keep a pet bird?

A bird makes the ideal first pet. It
● is easy to keep
● makes little mess
● does not have any real smell
● is cheap to buy and even cheaper to keep
● occupies very little space

What is more, all the species covered in this book will breed in cages. This means you can make your own contribution to conservation. Birds are sometimes specially bred by experts for releasing into the wild. This, of course, is possible only if there are enough birds in captivity. The knowledge needed to do this is built up by people encouraging their birds to breed.

Even birds seemingly common in the wild can face a sudden threat from which they seem to have no protection. The wild population of the Gouldian Finch, possibly the most beautiful bird in the world, is dwindling due to a sudden attack from a virus. The bird seems to have no natural defenses against it. Many people in this country have bred the Gouldian Finch for years. Therefore it is unlikely to become completely extinct.

Why is keeping a bird, or birds, so popular? The pace and demands of living are constantly increasing. Many people feel that watching TV or playing with computers is not everything in life. The question is, what else is there to do?

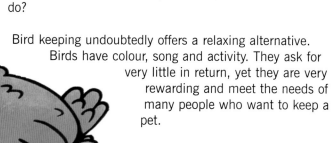

Bird keeping undoubtedly offers a relaxing alternative. Birds have colour, song and activity. They ask for very little in return, yet they are very rewarding and meet the needs of many people who want to keep a pet.

Also, our feathered friends take up very little room. This means they are suitable where there isn't much space for other pets – where the garden is not really big enough for a dog, or four-legged pets are banned, as they are in many blocks of flats.

Which bird should I keep?

Birds are as different from one another as people. Some birds require specialist care and are not suitable for beginners. This still leaves many other birds from which you can choose.

The first question is, where are you going to put the cage? A pair of birds (a cock and a hen) will be quite happy by themselves. They can be kept in a bedroom, spare room or even in a frost-free and well-lit shed or garage.

A family area, such as a living room, is also fine. But make sure there is not too much smoke, no sudden or loud noises, or draughts. Birds have more sensitive lungs and hearing than humans and a draught or sudden change in temperature can be a real killer.

Our feathered friends are tolerant creatures, except when they are nesting. Then they do require peace and quiet and the minimum of interruptions. The hen gets fed up if she is disturbed often and will not incubate (keep warm) the eggs.

Not every species of bird likes being by itself. However, some will accept humans as company. A single cock budgerigar will 'adopt' you. With a little patience it will also become tame, learn to talk and be a member of the family. Hens do not normally talk much, if at all.

A cock canary, given a little company, will also be quite happy without a partner. It will sing away to let the world know it is there.

Did you know?

Charles Coxon, the brother-in-law of John Gould, was probably the first person to breed the budgerigar in captivity.

Foreign Finches give you activity, colour and song. They hate being without a mate and will not accept a human as substitute. With some finches, it may be difficult to tell which sex is which. There is one golden rule for these and other species. If in doubt, keep true pairs (cock and hen) or just hens. Two cocks may fight, and seriously injure or kill one another. This is due to the way birds behave in the wild. It is the cock's job to establish a territory and provide food for the hen and the chicks. His instinct is to fight off other males, even if there is no hen around. The cock sings to advertise his presence. It is the hen's job to find the cock. As a result her calls tend to be in the form of an 'answer', letting him know there is a hen nearby.

Time? Space? Cost?

These questions are very easy to answer. Just a few minutes a day are all that are needed to check your bird's basic needs (food, water, grit and cuttlefish bone) and replenish them as necessary. Keeping the cage clean is normally a once-a-week job.

The amount of space required in the cage you buy depends on whether you are going to breed your birds. A guide to sizes and dimensions of suitable cages is given in chapter 4.

Did you know:
A canary is often bred with a goldfinch or greenfinch. An offspring from such a couple is called a 'mule'.

None of the birds is expensive to buy and all are cheap to feed. The principal (but not sole) part of their diet is seed. This is readily available from local stores, pet shops and many markets.

Half a kilogram (1lb) of Foreign Finch Seed should last six Foreign Finches at least a couple of weeks! How long will it last a pair? You can work that one out...!

Chapter 2

Choosing your bird

The cheerful budgerigar

At the moment, the budgerigar is probably the most popular cage bird in Great Britain, although the canary, the holder of the No 1 spot for hundreds of years, is making a determined comeback.

Did you know?

The Aboriginal name for the budgerigar was Betcherygah, meaning 'good bird'.

The parrot family is noted for its ability to talk and learn tricks.

The budgie has been known to live for more than 20 years, although its normal lifespan is six to eight years. Any of the species in this book can be remarkably long lived. In the wild, a bird has many natural enemies and, as a result, its lifespan tends to be short. In captivity, it has only a friend, you. Thus it will live a lot longer.

The reasons for the budgie's enormous popularity are not hard to find. As a pet or first bird it has so much to offer. A single budgerigar makes a hardy, tolerant and cheerful companion. It is a happy and active bird which can be taught to 'talk'. Even if kept only as a companion, and not taught to talk, a budgie still chatters away happily.

To be technically correct, budgies mimic sounds rather than actually talk. The cock bird is best at doing this. Not many hens talk, no matter how hard their owners try to teach them.

The budgie is a member of the parrot family. Like other members of this family, the budgie is an intelligent bird.

Did you know?

Immature birds of many species are often difficult to sex.

A pair of budgies opens up the door marked 'breeding' and the fascinating world which lies behind.

The difference between the sexes is easy to spot in mature budgerigars. The cere of the male is blue whilst that of the female is brown. Mature birds have a 'necklace' of black spots around the bottom half of the throat.

It was because the budgie was easy to breed that early bird keepers liked to keep it. However, little did they realise the treasure trove of varieties they were unlocking.

There are now well over 20 main types to choose from. These include pink-eyed, crested and fringed birds. Those most frequently sold in pet shops are the normal (green) and blue varieties. However, there are other ways to buy your budgie as well as from a pet shop, and this is explained further in chapter 3.

male   female

There are currently over 100 different 'colour schemes' and lots more are still possible. So if you take up breeding budgies you might 'invent' another and become famous!

The budgie clambers about its cage on its ladders, and plays with bells or toys. It has much in common with humans – especially when it admires itself in a mirror!

Did you know?
The wild budgie is predominantly green but 'yellow' ones can sometimes be seen.

The singing canary

Have you ever been to the Canary Islands for a holiday? If so, did you see a dull green bird with quite a pleasant song? This is the original canary from which all today's canaries are descended, whatever their colour.

There are at least a dozen different varieties and many different colours. Each breed has an interesting history. The canary with the best song has historically been the Roller.

The Roller has a lovely, soft, though somewhat short, song. Roller-singing contests are held in many areas of Europe. The winners are highly prized and used to teach young Rollers to sing.

Did you know?
A pair of cage birds both possessing artificially created crests or fringes produce weak and sickly offspring.

The Gloster was bred into existence by keen fanciers in the 1920s. It comes both with a fringe and without one. The fringed bird is called the Crested Gloster. If it does not have a fringe it is known simply as the (ordinary) Gloster. In a breeding pair, one bird will be fringed and one plain. The one with a fringe is called the Corona and the one without, the Consort.

With or without a fringe, the Gloster is a common bird at canary and bird exhibitions or shows.

The Gloster is a quick mover and full of life. It is also easy to get the bird used to strangers peering at it. Therefore it makes an ideal bird to own when the cage has to be hung where lots of different people are always coming and going.

Another canary popular amongst canary fanciers is the Fife – also a good choice for beginners. There is a picture of a Fife in **Useful addresses**.

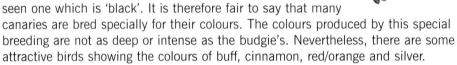

Ordinary (left) and Crested Gloster (right).

Some of the more 'specialist' canaries have fluffy feathers giving the appearance of a frill (the Frilled canary).

Not all canaries, even within the same variety, are yellow. Indeed, I have even seen one which is 'black'. It is therefore fair to say that many canaries are bred specially for their colours. The colours produced by this special breeding are not as deep or intense as the budgie's. Nevertheless, there are some attractive birds showing the colours of buff, cinnamon, red/orange and silver.

This isn't bad from what originally was a dull, olive-green bird, albeit one which has given so much pleasure to people for hundreds of years!

The colourful and cheerful Foreign Finches

These birds have, on more than one occasion, been described as 'coloured gems'. Active and colourful, the group contains some of the easiest of birds to keep and breed, and they are not necessarily expensive.

Foreign Finches do not sing like canaries. Rather, they have a series of pleasant, twittering calls. The reason for this can be found in nature.

Did you know?

The Zebra Finch has over a dozen separate calls.

The Zebra Finch comes from Australia. It lives in flocks of up to 100 birds.

Most finches live in a flock for the greater part of the year. This means that the cock does not need to sing to attract a mate at breeding time. The pair has met already as part of normal, day-to-day flock living. The sounds flock birds make tend to be of a pleasant, background nature, hence the earlier use of the word 'twittering'. The aim is that everyone in the flock keeps in touch.

As a bird keeper, you will notice that the 'calls' of a Foreign Finch serve a specific purpose. Perhaps it is warning of your arrival in the room!

The term 'Foreign' Finches or birds is to some extent misleading. All the birds covered in this book are foreign, that is, not native (British) by origin but they have all been bred successfully in this country for many years.

There is no doubt that the Zebra Finch makes an ideal bird for a beginner. Its patterns of behaviour are typical of many of the birds kept in cages. A pair of Zebra Finches is an excellent example of bird life for you to study and learn about birds. Even better, Zebras are easily available and inexpensive!

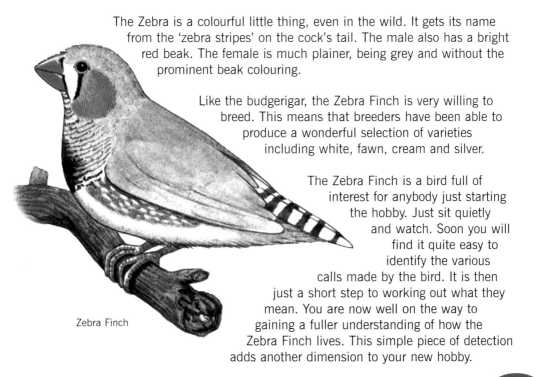

The Zebra is a colourful little thing, even in the wild. It gets its name from the 'zebra stripes' on the cock's tail. The male also has a bright red beak. The female is much plainer, being grey and without the prominent beak colouring.

Like the budgerigar, the Zebra Finch is very willing to breed. This means that breeders have been able to produce a wonderful selection of varieties including white, fawn, cream and silver.

The Zebra Finch is a bird full of interest for anybody just starting the hobby. Just sit quietly and watch. Soon you will find it quite easy to identify the various calls made by the bird. It is then just a short step to working out what they mean. You are now well on the way to gaining a fuller understanding of how the Zebra Finch lives. This simple piece of detection adds another dimension to your new hobby.

Zebra Finch

Another popular bird is the Bengalese Finch. It is unique in one respect, having been created entirely by man. Unlike the canary or budgerigar, it is not a development from a specific wild bird. Nobody really knows for sure how, when or where it came about. The best guess is that it originated as a fertile hybrid of two other finches and/or a mannikin. The Bengalese seems to have originated somewhere in the Far East many hundreds of years ago.

What is certain is its peaceful, sociable nature. I have never known one to be otherwise. An alternative name is the Society Finch. In short, it is a complete 'softy'.

Bengalese enthusiasts have developed other attractive forms of the bird such as chocolate and white, fawn and white, and crested chocolate. All these varieties stem from the normal variety of chestnut and white.

> ### Did you know?
> *The Zebra Finch was first classified scientifically by John Gould 160 years ago.*

For a beginner who wants a bird with a pleasant disposition, the Bengalese Finch is hard to beat.

Many people whose first birds were Foreign Finches have found them alluring and addictive. The birds they originally bought as an introduction to a hobby have become a permanent feature of their lives. Dainty, active and colourful, with characters of their own, the Bengalese and Zebra Finches are ideal for the novice.

Bengalese Finch

Chapter 3

Buying your bird

Congratulations! You know the sort of bird you want to keep and why. The next important step is to buy from the best source. This ensures your purchase will be a fit and healthy bird.

Where should I buy?

There are three main sources from which you can buy a bird:

- pet shops
- breeders
- from people advertising in the paper

Wherever you live, there should be a pet shop or breeder not too far away.

Buying birds 'by mail' should be left to the experienced bird keeper who knows the right questions to ask in advance. It is too late to realise you have made a mistake after you have bought the cage and the bird arrives. Exchanges or refunds are difficult in cases like this. Answering an advertisement in the local paper is a different matter.

There are many advantages in buying in your own area. For a start, you might want to breed, when it is much better to have an unrelated pair. When you have seen some birds you like, just ask the breeder, 'Can you let me have an unrelated pair?' This is important, because chicks bred from a pair which is closely related tend to be weak, sickly and/or deformed, do not normally live long and are unsuitable for further breeding.

When you visit the pet shop or breeder, have a good look around. What general impression do the birds and accommodation make? Is everything clean and tidy? Are the people helpful?

Did you know?

Cage & Aviary Birds, *the weekly magazine for the bird keeper, has lots of 'small ads' of birds for sale. Some of these could be near you.*

Wherever you buy from, the bird should be alert, lively, clean and with 'tight' plumage. If birds are housed together, take time to check that the one you want is neither a weakling nor a bully. Do not buy a bird if it has:

- a dull, listless, sulky look
- missing toes, swollen feet or cannot perch properly
- a discharge from the nasal tubes
- a soiled vent

Do not be soft and buy a bird at a 'bargain price' if it doesn't look well. It is just not worth it. The poor thing will probably die shortly after you get it home. It should not have been on sale either; such birds give people a totally false impression of the hobby. So the mark of a good shop or breeder is that all the birds on sale are fit, lively and healthy.

Try to find a pet shop which specialises in birds and go along when it is not too busy. The owner can then devote more time to you. If the shop is crowded, the birds will probably be fluttering about, upset by all the activity. A sick bird may then seem the same as a fit one for the short time you have to look at it. So try to avoid buying when there are lots of people about.

If you are inexperienced, it is also a good choice to go to a local breeder of your favoured species. There are many reasons for this.

The breeder will be able to devote more time to you. After all, you've both got the same hobby. He'll give you lots of advice, hints and information. You will find many bird club members are also keen breeders (see chapter 10, Joining a bird club).

Did you know?
Pet shops and bird dealers are listed in Yellow Pages and Thomsons directories.

A breeder may sell some birds more cheaply than others. There is a good reason for this – the breeder does not think they will win any show prizes. However, some of the faults are so small that only another expert would notice them.

When is the best time to buy?

All the birds mentioned in this book can be bought at any time of the year. All are domesticated – none are imported. The best time to buy is in the autumn when prices should be at their lowest. This is because many birds are available which have been bred through the previous months.

Birds born in the current year should be mature enough to be sexed by the autumn. If you want to buy a pair, you should be able to use them to breed the following year. Young birds also settle down and adapt to a new routine more quickly.

Getting the birds home

A pet shop or a breeder is likely to put the birds in a cardboard box designed for the purpose. Make sure you do not block the ventilation holes by mistake on the journey home. These boxes, although not particularly strong and robust, are fine for a trip of not more than a couple of hours. Anything longer and you really need something better than a box.

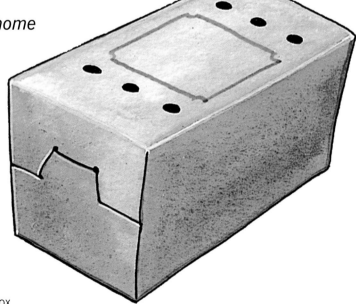

Small birds have to eat regularly and they need light to do this. One solution is to carry them home in a cage so that you can sprinkle seed on the floor. This is particularly convenient if you get both cage and bird together (see chapter 4, Housing your bird).

It is always a good idea to find out what seed or mix the bird is accustomed to and take some home with you. You will then know what your new friend is used to and likes. It all helps the bird to settle down quickly in strange surroundings. Some birds need time to be introduced gradually to a new seed diet.

What happens next?

As soon as you get home, put the cage in its permanent position. If it is dark by this time, give the bird a couple of hours of artificial light so that it can fill its crop (feed) before roosting for the night. It is most important for a small bird to be given time to fill its crop before it goes to sleep. A small bird with an empty crop may not last the night.

Did you know?

The crop of a bird is where digestion of seed starts on its way to the stomach.

After two or three weeks a bird should be used to its new surroundings and routine. Use this time wisely. Experienced bird keepers keep a close eye on their new charges for this period. They ask themselves many questions:

- are the birds healthy, fit and active?
- am I feeding them correctly?
- are they the right sex?

None of the birds in this book are difficult to buy. There are literally millions of them in this country.

Wherever you obtain your birds, people will be as helpful to you as they can. Remember, try to go along when the seller is not too busy. This helps to make sure you get the bird you want in a fit and healthy state.

Did you know?

In bird advertisements, EB means English Bred, BB British Bred and S/S Surgically Sexed.

Chapter 4

Housing your bird

There are a large number of cage styles and designs on the market but you do not have to be confused by the variety. This chapter will help you to make the correct choice.

Getting the right cage is just as important from your bird's point of view as it is to your enjoyment of the hobby. A properly-housed bird is a happy bird. A happy bird is a fit and healthy one which will repay you with hours of pleasure and interest. The reward will be especially satisfying at breeding time. If you buy a pair you will probably want to breed, so make sure the cage of your choice is the right one. This is explained later in the chapter.

As you become more experienced, you will have clearer ideas of how you want to progress. You may even want to build an aviary to give your birds conditions which are as close to nature as possible.

Type of cage

There are two main types of cage: the fancy wire cage, or the plywood, box-type cage. The former is just about suitable for the single pet bird such as a canary or budgerigar providing, that is, the cage is rectangular in design. If it is dome-shaped, the bird may not be able to exercise properly. It is helicopters which can fly up and down, not cage birds!

The box-type cage, made from plywood with a wire front, is infinitely preferable and often cheaper. It gives the bird a sense of security, and additional privacy when breeding.

> **Did you know?**
> The words 'cage' and 'aviary' come from the Latin words cavea and aviarium. Respectively, these mean 'enclosure' and 'a place where birds are kept'.

Any of the birds covered by this book live quite happily in such a cage. These cages are known as single-, double- or triple-breeders, depending on the number of compartments. Compartments in a double- or triple-breeder can be separated by a divider.

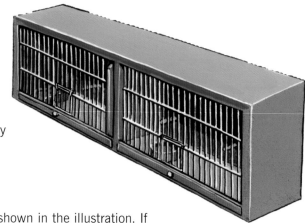

The best choice is probably a double-breeder because it gives you that little bit of temporary, extra space which comes in useful for breeding. The birds can also be shut up in one half of the cage while you clean the other, which they much prefer.

Cage fronts

A typical example of a cage front is shown in the illustration. If someone gives you a cage you may find the front is made of mesh. This is typical of home-made cages. Whatever sort of cage you get, make sure the wire is sound, clean and free of rust. There should be no sharp edges on which you or the birds can injure yourselves.

Decide on the species of bird you want before buying a cage. This way you can check that:

● it is big enough
● you can use the right nest box for your birds if you are going to breed
● the gaps between the wires do not allow the bird to get its head stuck or even to escape

A small bird can squeeze through a remarkably small gap. I once had a female Golden Breasted Waxbill which could wriggle between parallel wires through which I could only just poke my little finger!

Did you know?

The Golden Breasted Waxbill (Estrilda sublava) is one of the smallest of all cage birds. It grows only to 90–95mm (3.5–3.75in).

Perches

Perches are made out of plastic, wood dowelling or natural wood. I prefer natural wood but I will tell you about each sort so you can make up your own mind.

Plastic perches are very easy to clean. However, many birds like to use their perch to keep their beaks in trim. Wood dowelling meets this need, is easy to clean and relatively smooth. Natural wood, on the other hand, has lots of nooks and crannies in the bark which interest a bird, but it is not so easy to keep clean.

Did you know?
A bird's beak is made from keratin. This is the same natural material as in your hair and nails. It is always growing, which is why a bird needs to trim its beak constantly.

Did you know?
The laburnum tree is poisonous to both birds and humans.

I find that perches made from apple, plum or blackthorn wood are always well received by my birds. A budgerigar, for instance, enjoys stripping the bark. You may need to fix a natural wood perch in the cage by buying a perch holder. Make sure that any natural wood you use is not poisonous.

The diameter of the perch should be thick enough to ensure the bird's feet do not go all the way round. If the diameter is too small, the front claws will dig into the back of the foot. The result is an unhappy bird with sore feet.

Right

Wrong

Alternatively, a perch which is too thick stretches the bird's feet, preventing it from gripping the perch properly. Ideally you want a selection of perches, at varying heights and of different thicknesses, which will give variety.

The gap between perches should be as wide as possible. The bird then gets exercise by hopping or flying. When a bird is perched normally, its tail should not brush against the side or back of the cage.

Did you know?
A Zebra Finch, if it wants to, can hop almost 60cm (2ft) without really having to fly!

Constantly landing on a firmly-fixed perch is the same to a bird as you or me jumping up and down on concrete. The perch should be fixed so there is just a little 'spring' as the bird lands.

Cage base

This should have a sliding tray, preferably with handles. You need to cover the bottom of the tray, and there are a variety of floor coverings you can use to make cleaning easy.

Bird sand and sanded sheets are both suitable. The sand may well contain many useful minerals and trace elements and act as a source of grit. However, both of these can be expensive to buy. In any event, the minerals and trace elements should be provided as part of the normal diet (see chapter 5, Feeding your bird).

Sawdust is more likely to be used by specialist bird keepers for birds such as softbills which are messier in their habits than seed eaters.

Did you know?

'Softbill' is a generic term for any cage and aviary bird which does not feed mostly on seed. The principal part of its diet could be fruit or insects. A blackbird is an example.

To my mind, the best covering for the floor of the cage is the cheapest of the lot, old newspaper. It is also very absorbent. You can cut a complete paper to size easily to provide several weeks' supply at one go!

The cage should have an 8cm (3in) strip of wood or glass immediately above the tray. This helps to stop feathers, seeds and husks spilling into the room.

Buying a cage

The average size of a double-breeder is 91cm long x 41cm deep x 51cm high (36in x 16in x 20in). Length is the most important of the dimensions. The longer the cage the better, as this gives the birds more opportunity for exercise.

Buy a cage from the same source as the bird (see chapter 3, Buying your bird) or a specialist supplier (see Useful addresses). If you buy a second-hand cage, give it a good clean before putting in your bird (see chapter 6, General management).

Getting the cage ready

Wherever you get your cage, try to buy it before you get your bird. It can then be made ready to welcome your new friend on arrival.

Did you know?

Lead in paint is just as harmful to birds as it is to humans.

The inside of a double-breeder cage looks much better if it is coated with white emulsion. This is not poisonous to birds. The outside will look really smart if you brush on a coat of non-poisonous fence or shed preservative. I think the cedar red shade gives the nicest effect. Applying emulsion

and preservative is much easier, quicker and cheaper than painting. Allow plenty of time for the emulsion or preservative to dry before introducing the birds.

Siting the cage

Your bird is totally reliant on you for the world which surrounds it. The cage needs plenty of light

Did you know?

The ultra-violet rays in sunlight falling on a bird's plumage trigger off natural synthesis of Vitamin D3.

whilst at the same time being protected from draughts and the direct rays of the sun. Birds cannot stand direct sunlight for very long so make sure that, after a quick sunbathe, they can cool off by hopping back into the shade.

You can put the cage almost anywhere which is convenient, as long as it is on a firm base and not too close to the ground. This is especially important if there are other pets in the house. A position near a well-lit window is ideal. Try to avoid putting the cage where someone entering the room comes between the birds and the light from the window. This causes the birds to get nervous and agitated, as does loud noise.

Chapter 5

Feeding your bird

Overall, diet is the most important part of your bird-keeping activities. A good diet can turn a tatty-looking bird into one bouncing with life, health and vitality. Poor feeding can literally kill a bird. A bird's menu needs to be balanced and varied. A little forethought will pay generous dividends.

Birds in the wild are great dietary opportunists; they have to be to survive. This instinct has not been lost by cage birds, which makes it easy for you to provide a varied menu.

Did you know?
Unlike herbivores or carnivores, omnivores tend to have fairly simple gut systems, with lots of different microbes to digest all the different foods they eat.

All the birds in this book are seedeaters. They will also eat greenfood, softfood and, on occasions, livefood. They can therefore be regarded, to a greater or lesser degree, as omnivores, like many other birds.

Feeding the right food is the key to success. This chapter will help you do this cheaply.

Seed

Each species of bird in this book has its own, commonly-available seed mix. Zebra and Bengalese Finches eat Foreign Finch Seed Mix, budgerigars consume Budgerigar Seed Mix and canaries enjoy Canary Seed Mix.

There are two sorts of Canary Seed Mix: plain or mixed. I feed my canaries mostly on plain. A canary may get fat if it is fed entirely on mixed and a fat bird can become out of sorts and won't breed well.

The cheapest way to buy bird seed is from your local pet or pet food shop. It is also available from many Corn and Agricultural Merchants. Your seed will probably be sold both loose (the cheapest) and pre-packed. It is not really worth the bother of buying the individual seeds and making your own 'mixes'. Normally, only bird keepers with a large number of birds find this worth their while.

All seed should have an oily sheen. This means it is fresh and full of food value, so avoid buying cheap, dull-looking seed.

Equipment

All seed should be stored in air-tight containers. Clear plastic bottles (of the type containing squash or cordial) hold 0.45kg (1lb), enough to last a pair of birds some weeks. Thoroughly clean the inside, allow to dry and pour the seed into the bottle using a funnel. You will then find the seed easy to dish out accurately without making a mess.

A wide variety of feeding equipment is available. For a small number of birds, probably the best is the 'Flomatic' type. This is suitable for water or seed and is secured to the wire or mesh of the cage with a plastic or metal clip. When full, it contains enough water or seed to last several days.

> **Did you know?**
> *You can easily identify Canary from Foreign Finch Seed Mix. Canary Seed tends to be oval rather than round.*

> **Did you know?**
> *Millet seed forms the basis of the mixes eaten by smaller birds. Millet is a cereal grass, just like the wheat grown for bread making.*

> **Did you know?**
> *Cage and aviary birds are classified as seedeaters (also known as hardbills), softbills, carnivores and nectar feeders.*

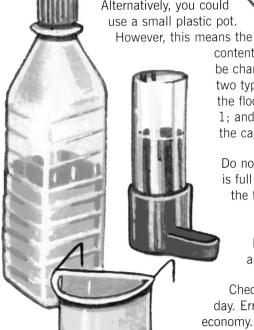

Alternatively, you could use a small plastic pot. However, this means the contents have to be changed every day. There are two types of pot: those which stand on the floor of the cage as illustrated in chapter 1; and the sort which hangs on the wire of the cage as shown in this illustration.

Do not believe the pot or hanging container is full because you think you can see seed on the top. It could well be only seed husks. Gently blow these away and you will see there is probably very little seed left, certainly not enough to last another 24 hours.

Check the levels of seed and water every day. Err on the side of caution rather than economy. To be safe, I always make sure there is enough to last two days rather than one.

Other sorts of seed

Sprouted or germinating seed is especially high in vitamin content and is very easy to prepare. Find an old, clean margarine or spread tub. Put some fresh seed into the tub

and cover it with water. The seed will start to germinate between one and five days depending on the temperature and time of year.

Each day you need to drain, rinse and change the water. This prevents the seed going off. Smell the seed after you drain it. If it is off, there will be a musty smell.

The seed is ready when it has a very small 'tail', showing that germination

has started. Ideally the length of the tail should be about 1–2mm (0.10in). If in doubt, take a few seeds out and look at them under a magnifying glass or microscope. All you need to do now is to rinse it thoroughly once or twice and serve in a separate container.

The heads of wild seeding grasses in the summer make a welcome addition to any bird's menu, but you must make sure they are clean. You should not use grasses from the roadside, as they are likely to have been polluted by pesticides and car fumes. Similarly, make sure that any grasses from the garden have not been contaminated by weedkillers or soiled by domestic animals.

Millet sprays, available from pet shops, are eagerly consumed by our feathered friends. The spray is the dried seed head of the millet plant.

Did you know?

A germinating seed manufactures and releases vitamins over and above the nutritional value already there.

Greenfood

Greenfood is a valuable source of
vitamins and trace elements. You can
choose from a wide variety of plants.
Greenfood should be provided at least
once a week.

The following are all suitable: dandelion,
groundsel, lettuce and brussel sprout leaves.
Shredded carrot is a valuable source of
Vitamin A. Spinach is suitable only
in small portions as it contains a
tiny amount of oxalic acid which is
poisonous to birds.

Rhubarb leaves contain a lot of
oxalic acid and should be
completely avoided. Cabbage is
also best left alone. It can depress
thyroid gland activity and/or, in
some cases, cause constipation.
Greenfood needs to be washed clean
and be free from any contaminants
before being fed to the birds. Small
birds appreciate the leaves being
chopped or cut into small pieces. A
complete leaf should be young and
tender, otherwise your bird may not have
enough strength in its beak to eat it!

Make sure any greenfood taken from
the fridge, or from outside in
winter, is not frosted. This is a
common cause of avian tummy upsets.

Softfood

There are two sorts of softfood: the one you buy and the one you make yourself. The
most suitable one you can buy for your birds is probably egg food. Normally it is
available both loose and pre-packed. Mix the egg food with a little water until it is
crumbly and moist, when you can give it to the birds.

A cheap and easy dish to make at home consists of two common domestic foodstuffs:
bread and milk. Cut a small amount of white bread into cubes, soak in a little milk

until moist and then serve. However, do check after a few hours that the milk has not gone sour, especially in hot weather.

Don't despair if it takes your birds a few days to get used to softfood. They may not have been offered it before: a bird's parents can only teach it what to eat if the food is there. Usually, birds are taught by their parents what is good food and what is bad. They do not make the distinction instinctively.

Did you know?
Flintstone grit lasts a long time in the bird. Oystershell is mostly softer lime which breaks down quickly to release its minerals.

A good supply of softfood, checked and topped up regularly, is essential when birds are breeding.

Grit

Grit is an indispensable part of your bird's diet and should always be available. Flintstone grit helps the bird to break down the seed in its gizzard before proper digestion starts. It also contains minerals valuable in egg and bone formation. Buy ready-mineralised grit but, if it is not available in this form, you can add some powdered oystershell.

Cuttlefish bone

Cuttlefish bone is another basic item sold by your local pet shop. It is full of calcium essential for both bone strength and good egg production. It can be fixed to the front of the cage with a cuttlefish bone clip.

Did you know?
The cuttlefish is a member of the Cephalopod family which possesses the most highly developed nervous and sensory system of all invertebrates.

Fruit

Again the choice is wide and varied. What your birds eat is down to their personal preferences as much as anything else. You can chop an apple into small pieces for them to peck at. A juicy orange segment might be a bit messy but provides interesting 'afters'. My birds also find a piece of mango, plum or banana equally worthy of their consideration.

You must soak dried fruit properly before giving it to your bird. Anything dried (including bread) may swell up in the bird's stomach as it absorbs the digestive juices. This causes the bird severe discomfort and could even kill it.

Other things

If asked, I am sure my birds would say they are mystified why the 'finger biscuits' they eat so willingly are called 'Canary biscuits'. After all, they all like them, even the small parrots.

> ### Did you know?
>
> *Unlike fresh fruit, dried fruit contains no Vitamin C. It is all destroyed in the drying process.*
>
> *Vitamin A helps to protect birds against digestive infections.*

In winter, you can add a couple of drops of Cod Liver Oil to dry seed each week to provide extra Vitamins A and D.

When you have only a small number of birds, live food can prove expensive. However, as you get to know other bird keepers, you may find there are local sources you can take advantage of.

Various treats, tonics and tonic seeds are readily available in the shops. If the bird's diet is good, then there really should be no need for them.

For a bird, the simplest thing may be a treat. For example, most of my birds complain loudly if I forget to give them their daily ration of soaked seed!

Chapter 6

General management

Looking after birds is just like life itself. If you start by doing the correct thing, you stand a good chance of staying on the right path.

Some details of bird keeping may seem to be less important than others, but this does not lessen their value to the bird. Ignoring them could easily reduce the length of a bird's life.

When your birds are moved to your home, they suffer a traumatic experience. The first things they need are food, water, and peace and quiet for a couple of hours.

Did you know?
Vitamin D3, naturally synthesised by a bird, helps it to move calcium around its body to where it is needed.

After three or four days your birds should have become accustomed to you and settled down. So start off by adopting a regular feeding and cleaning routine. After all, I am sure you like to be fed at the same time each day!

Also, sit down and quietly watch your birds for a few minutes every day. You will notice, much to your pleasure, that each bird has its own personality. Your hobby will be so much more rewarding if you observe (not just look), listen and learn to pick up avian 'messages'.

The first question I always ask when a problem arises is 'what have I done wrong?', not think 'stupid birds'. You may only be able to work out a solution if you understand your birds and how they think.

Bird think

Your birds have eyes at the side of their heads. As a result, they cannot judge speed and distance very well. This is why so many small birds get killed on the roads. You, on the other hand, have eyes at the front of your head and can judge speed and distance very well. To a bird, this also means you are a predator, that is, a threat. It is your job to convince your birds that you are not a predator. Their feelings of fear will be reinforced if people arrive close by without warning. Always give notice of your approach with a soft whistle, or by using the same word of warning each time.

Did you know?
If an approaching vehicle gives a warning toot on the horn it is less likely to kill a bird on the road.

Handling

In the wild a bird can flee in flight, but not when it is in a cage. This is why a bird gets so frightened when it has to be caught. Never forget that however a bird is caught, it is probably the most distressing experience it suffers in its life. Therefore it is one which should not be repeated unnecessarily.

A bird can literally die from sheer fright after being caught, even a day or two later. Years ago, I had a female Zebra Finch that feigned death every time she was caught. The first time it happened I put her down sadly and sat down. That was a mistake. An eye opened, away she flew and I had to catch her again. Fortunately she survived what must have been a double dose of trauma!

Did you know?
A bird's skeleton is built for lightness in flight, not for strength.

You need calmness plus a sure and steady (yet speedy) hand. A bird is a fragile little creature which should never be caught in flight. Wait until it is on the floor or wire of the cage and carefully put your hand around it.

The correct way to hold a small bird is to have its back against your palm with its head poking out between your first and second fingers which should be gently gripping the neck. This makes sure your bird will not escape. If you hold the head between the first finger and thumb, a small bird may wriggle free and escape. To be safe, always close doors and windows before you catch a bird.

Alternatively you could buy a net specially designed for catching birds and keep it for emergencies. To avoid injury, make sure the diameter of the net is slightly larger than the wingspan of your birds. You should never catch a bird in flight either by hand or net.

Did you know?
Your ability to see is better in low light levels than your bird's. This gives you an advantage.

If a bird does escape, the first thing is quickly to check that the room is escape proof. Secondly, draw the curtains or find some other way of reducing the light level. The bird is then likely to stay still and be caught more easily.

Cleaning

Your bird's cage should never smell. If it does, neither the occupants nor cage are being looked after properly. Just a few minutes each week are all that are required. You need:

- hot soapy water and a cleaning rag
- small dustpan (or substitute) and brush
- scissors to cut paper used for floor covering
- a small paintbrush or old toothbrush to get seed out of any nooks and crannies

It is now that a double breeder comes into its own. You can use the divider to keep the birds in one half while you clean the other. Remove the tray, dispose of the paper and waste, wipe the tray clean and cover it with fresh newspaper. You can then brush the cage clear of any seed and husks using the paint brush for the stubborn corners. Finally, wipe the inside clean, paying special attention to the perches.

Do not use a vacuum cleaner to clean the cage. There is always the real danger that the bird you didn't realise was there will be sucked into the dustbag.

> **Did you know?**
>
> *The word 'Abracadabra', written in a triangle and worn by the patient, was originally supposed to cure fevers.*

The birds can then change sides and the procedure repeated. Abracadabra, and it's finished!

Mites and bacteria, harmful to birds, hide in the cracks and joins of the cage. At least once a year you need to sterilise the cage. You can buy a special avian disinfectant but follow the instructions carefully. If you can't buy an avian disinfectant, Jeyes Fluid (obtainable from most hardware/gardening outlets) is a good alternative.

Remove the birds, thoroughly clean the cage and use a solution of 1 part Jeyes Fluid to 80 parts of water (65ml in 5 litres). Rinse the cage and mop up excess liquid. Finally, allow the cage to dry and ventilate it thoroughly before returning the birds.

> **Did you know?**
>
> *John Jeyes first patented his Fluid in 1877.*

Feeding utensils should be cleaned every day. It is handy to have two sets; one can be in use whilst the other is cleaned to be ready for the next day.

Steady birds

Most of the birds at bird exhibitions seem relatively unconcerned by people peering at them. Such birds are known as 'steady'. Steady birds are a credit to their owner.

Some of your visitors may have the habit of putting their faces near to the cage wire. This is likely to frighten a bird not used to close inspection. It is easy to get a bird used to close contact. Speak softly, and gradually and repeatedly move your face closer to the front of the cage until the bird is used to it. Congratulations, you now have a steady bird!

Taming

If you have a single budgerigar as a companion and friend, naturally you will want to tame it. The other birds in this book are not suitable for taming and do not talk.

It is not difficult to get a budgie finger tame once it has become thoroughly used to you. Select a favourite titbit, such as a small piece of apple or carrot. Wedge this between the wires of the cage and watch the bird gradually pluck up courage to nibble at it.

Now you can accustom it to your hand in the cage. Place the titbit between your fingers, slowly put them in the cage within reach of the bird and keep still. After a while, the bird will approach your fingers and peck at the titbit.

If it pecks you, put yourself in the bird's shoes. The bird thinks you are trespassing in the only world it knows so is trying to defend its territory. It is your job to convince your bird that you are its friend. Never move suddenly or quickly. Always speak softly: why not say its name?

Eventually you will be able to put your finger in the cage without a titbit. After a few sessions the bird should allow you to stroke its belly immediately above the top of its legs. A little pressure there and the bird should involuntarily hop up onto your finger.

Birds let out of a cage know nothing of domestic hazards such as hot surfaces and liquids, chimneys, net curtains or clear panes of glass. You must make sure the room is completely safe and escape proof. For example, do not leave pot plants in the room – they may be poisonous. It is your responsibility to make sure your feathered friend is safe.

Did you know?
Nature tells a bird to flee when scared. This is why you should always check that windows are secure. Many birds are lost by escaping through open windows.

A talking budgie

You will probably want to teach your budgie to 'talk'. This is much easier if the bird is tame and young, but is not impossible with older birds. Only one person should do the training.

Did you know?
The budgerigar's ability to mimic was first discovered in Germany towards the end of the 19th century.

The trick is to repeat the word you want the budgie to learn every time you are near the cage, especially when you are about to feed the bird. Once this is mastered, you can move on to short phrases, slowly building up the bird's vocabulary.

Don't forget that each bird is an individual, just like you and me, and some learn to mimic more quickly than others. It is all a question of patience and persistence. Male budgies are more likely to talk than females.

Bathing

You should provide facilities for your birds to bathe two or three times a week all the year round. Make sure they have their bath early in the morning so they do not go to roost with damp feathers and get chilled. The best bathing receptacle is some form of small, low-sided dish. The sides should not be too high or the bath too full of water, otherwise a small bird or a chick, unable to get out easily, may panic and drown.

Chapter 7

Breeding: tips and hints

Congratulations on wanting to breed birds. You are the ideal conservationist. You plan to produce more than you consume!

Breeding should be the aim of all true bird keepers. There is not a limitless supply of birds, and it is possible that bird keepers may become the guardians of the only remaining examples of a species. The more people who breed birds, the better. This means many different species will flourish in captivity and the stock will be unrelated and strong.

> **Did you know?**
> Less than 200 years ago, the American Passenger Pigeon was the most numerous bird in the world. One flock could contain billions of birds. They were a favourite food of Americans in the 19th century.

All the species in this book are domesticated. This means they have quite cheerfully adapted to cage and/or aviary life. They should breed without difficulty, making you a true aviculturalist.

Diet (including grit and cuttlefish bone) is especially important. Why not sit down and work out a menu with a different, nutritious treat each day (see also chapter 6, Feeding your bird)? Do this a month before you intend to start your breeding programme and continue the special diet throughout the breeding period.

> **Did you know?**
> The last Passenger Pigeon, the weakened outcome of inbreeding, died in a zoo in 1914.

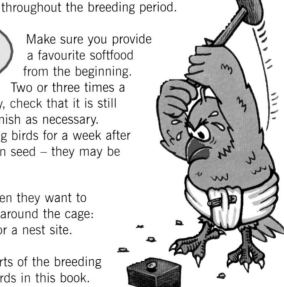

Make sure you provide a favourite softfood from the beginning. Two or three times a day, check that it is still fresh, and replenish as necessary. Continue supplying it to the young birds for a week after you think they can feed themselves on seed – they may be fooling you.

The birds themselves will tell you when they want to breed. You may see one bird peering around the cage: breeding instinct is telling it to look for a nest site.

This chapter tells you about those parts of the breeding cycle which are common to all the birds in this book.

Sexing

Normally it is easy to confirm you have a cock and hen. Divide your double breeder into two halves with a bird in each. The male should sing and the female respond, either by chirping and/or with her movements. Try it and see.

In the wild it is generally the hen's job to find the male and the cock's to establish suitable territory. Don't try to breed two pairs in the same cage: both males will consider it their patch.

Never keep two cocks together (with or without a hen). For example, two Zebra Finch males will fight and one will probably die. Similarly, two hens and a cock in the same cage can result in the unwanted hen being persecuted and killed. Serious disputes normally happen very early in the morning and by the time you have woken up, it is too late.

Did you know?

The youngest of the brood is most at risk immediately after separation from the parents.

Light

The length of the day is critical. If it is too short, there may not be enough time for the parents to feed their chicks properly. This results in weaklings destined for an early grave. Ideally aim for a day of at least 13 hours. You can use artificial light to achieve this. Make sure the light is switched on early in the morning. Never switch it off suddenly in the evening as the birds will be unable to return to their nest because of the unexpected darkness!

Did you know?

Only one of 15 or 16 chicks hatched by a wild pair of Zebra Finches each year may survive.

Nesting

Although not essential, two dividers are helpful when breeding: one of plywood (so that the birds cannot see the other half of the cage) and one of wire (so that they can). Get one bird in each half of the cage and insert the plywood divider. Leave this in place for five days, then replace it with the wire one for the last two days. You should see a definite increase in courtship activity.

Remove the wire divider as early in the day as possible and the birds should mate shortly afterwards. A couple of days after mating, place the nesting material in the cage. The exception to this is with budgerigars (see chapter 8).

That the cock feeds the hen during courtship does appear to have more meaning than just a gesture of affection. In avian terms, he is probably showing his ability and willingness to feed the young when they hatch. It far more exhausting for the hen to rear the chicks than to lay the eggs. Feeding her (or even attempting to) is therefore clearly significant to the hen.

> **Did you know?**
> *Both canary and budgerigar cocks feed their mates during courtship and breeding.*

Providing the proper nesting material (see chapter 8, Breeding: individual species) helps keep the eggs at the right temperature naturally. Avoid using:

- straw, for fear of deadly fungal spores
- twine, string, cotton, wool or anything which may trap a bird or chick

When the hen is happy with the nest she will lay her clutch of eggs and incubation will start. The birds must have peace and quiet. Too much disturbance and they will abandon their nest, so suspend the weekly cleaning for the breeding period.

> **Did you know?**
> *At temperatures below 12°C (54°F) the embryo of an egg may die.*

Inspecting the nest at every opportunity disturbs the birds for no good reason, so do it as little as possible. Find out when the birds leave the nest of their own accord. Never force a bird to leave the nest box. Use the plywood divider to separate the birds from the nest box, take a quick look and withdraw the divider.

A cold hen may suffer from egg-binding (see chapter 9, Looking after sick birds). The ideal site for the cage is therefore somewhere secluded, dry and warm.

Breeding failures

Even the best-laid plans do not always work out properly. Birds are no exception to this rule, but still you will have far more successes than failures.

> **Did you know?**
> *Infertile eggs are known as 'clear' eggs because you should be able to see through them against a reasonably strong light.*

Perhaps the most common cause of failure is infertile eggs. Did you separate the pair for a week to excite the birds and increase the chances of successful mating? Are your perches fixed properly (see chapter 4, Housing your bird)? Have you checked you have a cock and hen?

Another reason for failure is DIS (Dead In Shell), where the shell is too hard for the chick to break out: too dry an atmosphere may have hardened the shell. Did you forget to allow your birds to bathe and moisten the eggs naturally?

Number of clutches

Even if you have spare accommodation, raising two sets of chicks per pair each year should be the limit. It is much better for the birds (and you) to concentrate effort on raising two fit and healthy broods rather than trying to produce many chicks.

Even if the chicks appear healthy, more than two sets and wear and tear start to affect the parents. Excessive breeding produces weaker chicks and the possibility of one or both parents dying through sheer exhaustion.

Identifying chicks

All the chicks may look the same to you, so you need to know which one is which. Even if they are not the same it is very easy to forget the key details.

The way to tackle the problem is to ring the chicks. You can then record individual details of each bird against the number on the ring. There are two ways of ringing a bird and both are explained further in chapter 10.

Remember that a chick is very fragile. Whenever you handle a bird, do it gently and without pressure.

Chapter 8

Breeding: individual species

The budgerigar

Opinions vary on the best time to start breeding. Some people say February (even as early as St Valentine's Day), others March. The sensible time is March when the weather is milder and there is more natural daylight.

When the cock budgerigar is in peak breeding condition his cere is shiny blue and, similarly, the hen's is shiny brown.

Did you know?

St Valentine is the patron saint of lovers because his feast day (February 14) fell on the same day as an ancient pagan fertility festival.

Budgerigar nest boxes come in many designs but ideally should have a removable bottom (for easy cleaning) with a concave area to stop the eggs rolling around. No nesting material is required apart from a little coarse sawdust (preferably pine) sprinkled over the bottom of the nest box. The sawdust absorbs the wetness in the droppings and helps to keep the eggs in place.

Normally four or five eggs are laid over alternate days. The hen incubates for about three weeks and the eggs then hatch every other day.

The hen feeds the chicks with naturally-produced crop milk for the first ten days or so. After this the cock has more work to do as the young are weaned onto solid food. Hopefully, you will have seen him feeding the hen during incubation. Now he should be frequently hopping in and out of the nest box to feed the young.

At about five weeks the young are fully feathered and should be able to feed themselves. Unless you have a spare cage for the young, you should now remove the nest box to stop a second clutch of eggs being laid, hatched and reared. If this were to happen your accommodation would become overcrowded.

Budgerigars require very little extra food
whilst breeding. Each day you should
provide:

- their favourite soft food
- some millet sprays when the chicks
  start emerging from the nest box

*One of the wild budgie's favourite nesting
trees is the eucalyptus. A member of the same
tree family, the gum tree, grows in this
country.*

The canary

Opinions also vary on the best time to start breeding canaries. Late March to early April
seems to be the popular time.

The hen canary builds the nest. Canaries use a nest pan (preferably with a felt liner)
rather than a nest box. You can provide moss, coconut hair (or cow hair) or ask your
local pet shop for suitable pet bedding material. Your pet shop should be able to sell
you pre-packed canary nesting material.

The first egg is laid seven or eight days after the hen has completed
the nest. The normal size of a clutch is four eggs. Canary breeders
often remove each egg after it is laid and substitute it
with a dummy one. The real one is put in a small
cotton-wool-lined margarine or spread tub. This can be
kept near the cage, at the same constant temperature,
for easy access and convenience.

When the clutch is complete the real eggs are returned
to the hen for the 13 or 14-day incubation period. All
the chicks then hatch at the same time. Eggfood now
becomes an important element in helping the hen to rear the
chicks.

The chicks start leaving the nest when they are about three weeks old and should be
fully independent at five or six weeks. Unless you have spare accommodation, remove
the nest pan at this stage to avoid a second round and overcrowding.

Separate the male from the female at any time after mating if he worries the hen
and/or her young. Some breeders do this automatically once mating has taken place
but it is not really necessary unless the cock is behaving badly.

Foreign Finches

Both the Zebra and Bengalese Finches make excellent parents. Indeed, so highly is the
Bengalese regarded that it is often used as a foster-parent to hatch the eggs and rear
the young of other finch species.

You should be able to tell when a pair is ready to mate. In late March or early April, put a very small amount of hay in the cage. The male should pick it up in his beak and show signs of wanting to build a nest. Another sign is that a Zebra Finch hen 'fans' her tail as an indication she is ready to mate.

Eggs laid at other times of the year will not be fertile.

Did you know?

A hen hearing the call of a cock Zebra Finch may start laying eggs even in the winter.

A nest box is normally a 13cm (5in) wooden cube with a half-open front. An alternative is a nest basket.

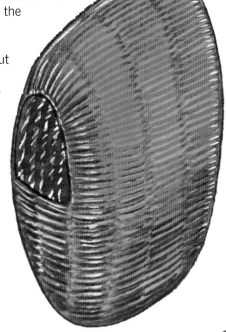

Egg laying starts 10–14 days after pairing. The cock uses most of this time to make the nest out of hay, seeding grasses and moss. Remove any spare nesting material once the hen is laying; a Zebra Finch cock may continue to nest-build and cover up the eggs.

Both parents share in the incubation, which is 12 days, and feeding the young. The young are fed on crop milk, naturally produced by the parents. It helps the birds make this if a favourite soft food is provided from the beginning of the breeding cycle.

The young leave the nest when they are about three weeks old but are still fed by their parents. Shortly after this, the chicks start to learn how to feed themselves, although they still beg for food from mum and dad!

At this stage, you must keep a close eye on the chicks: when the cock decides the time is right he will chase them away aggressively as he would in the wild. However, they cannot escape in a cage so they may suffer injury or even death as a result. Unless you have spare accommodation for the young, remove the nest box and separate the chicks from the adults with a divider for a few days.

Chapter 9

Looking after sick birds

Cage and aviary birds normally live longer than their wild counterparts. Even so, your bird's life is short compared to humans. This means a bird lives at a much faster pace.

At worst, a wild bird feeling off colour is likely to provide a tasty snack for a predator. At best, it will lose its place in the pecking order. Therefore, a bird strains every nerve to appear normal and so probably is in serious trouble by the time you notice that something is wrong.

Early action is essential. Always write down the symptoms in case you have to visit the veterinary surgeon. Why not find out who your nearest vet is and keep the number with your own personal ones?

Did you know?

In the wild, a Gouldian Finch is mature enough to breed at the age of 10–12 weeks.

Here are some of the signs which will tell you if you have a poorly bird.

The eyes should not be dull or appear sunken. The bird should not continually sleep in your presence.

How is its plumage? Regular preening keeps the bird looking sleek and shiny. A bird does not normally fluff up its feathers unless it is cold. It does, however, fluff up when it is ill and getting thin in order to make itself appear normal.

Is the bird's head tucked under a wing or buried in its chest feathers for long periods? Is its vent badly soiled? Finally, is its appetite normal?

Did you know?

In captivity a Zebra Finch can easily live for five years. In the wild it would be lucky to reach 18 months.

There are four things you should do when you think a bird is poorly. First, separate it from other birds. If you have not got a spare cage then, assuming you have a double breeder, use the plywood divider.

Second, make sure that you are giving the bird a good, nutritious and balanced diet (see chapter 5, Feeding your bird). This will increase its chances of survival.

Third, the bird should be fed last and everything used washed squeaky clean to avoid

Did you know?

The Swedish astronomer Anders Celsius (1701–44), who invented the Celsius (formerly Centigrade) temperature scale, originally had the freezing point of water at 100° and not 0°.

the spread of infection. Similarly, its cage should be thoroughly cleaned before the sick bird is isolated and again after it has recovered.

Last, warmth often allows the bird to cure itself. Ideally, the temperature needs to be initially maintained at 32°C (90°F) and then gradually reduced to 21°C (70°F) as recovery proceeds. The bird should then be allowed a few days so that you can check its recovery is complete before it is returned to its normal lifestyle.

The easiest way to provide the heat is with a thermostatically-controlled electric fan or other heater. Hot air rises, so take into account any difference in height between the thermostat and the cage.

The following alphabetical list covers some of the more common problems, but is not intended to be a comprehensive guide. If in doubt, the golden rule is: get advice quickly. Your bird may be only a hop away from death.

Beaks A bird whose beak requires trimming may not have been given the facilities for it to 'gnaw' something to keep its beak in good order. If you think a trim is necessary, consult a vet. Do not attempt it yourself.

Breathing If a bird is wheezing, gasping or has an open, gaping beak consult a vet without delay. It could be any one of a number of serious conditions. You can easily pick up the breathing pattern of a bird: every time it breathes, its tail will fall and rise slightly.

The symptom of Coryza (a respiratory infection) is a discharge from the nostrils and eyes. In bird terms, it is the equivalent of a human cold.

Generally, it is not fatal if it is treated promptly. Keep the patient warm and consult a vet if things do not improve in a day or so.

Breeding The hen should always have easy access to plentiful supplies of cuttlefish bone and grit and should not be allowed to breed when the temperature is too low (see chapters 7 and 8 on breeding). You should then have no problems. Some hens still unaccountably suffer from egg binding, which should not be confused with constipation. An egg-bound hen will:

- be on the floor of the cage
- have her feathers fluffed up
- be obviously straining to pass the egg

Hopefully, separating the bird and raising the temperature to 32°C (90°F) will work by itself within a short time. To be sure, you could catch the hen gently and smear her vent with glycerin. You must be gentle, otherwise you run the risk of crushing the egg inside the hen and killing her.

Do not breed with the hen until the next year and then give her special attention to avoid a repeat performance.

Broken leg or wing
see Limbs

Claws You should not have to trim your birds' claws provided that your perching arrangements are right. If you have to do it, get an experienced person to demonstrate the technique or pay a visit to the vet.

Colds and chills see Breathing

Conjunctivitis see Eyes

Constipation Constipation is a symptom rather than a disease in its own right.

The bird strains to produce droppings without much obvious success. The most likely cause is lack of greenfood in the diet and is easily remedied. Alternatively, a bird may concentrate on eating just one thing. I once kept a cockatiel which loved cabbage and a parrotlet which ate as much sunflower seed as it could.

The results? Constipation. The cures: I omitted cabbage from the menu of one (see also chapter 5, Feeding your bird) and rationed the sunflower seed for the other. I also added a few drops of olive oil to the seed and glycerin to the water for a week or so to help things on their way.

Constipation should not be confused with egg binding (see Breeding).

Diarrhoea This is marked by runny droppings and is often caused by poor diet. Is something in the diet 'off'? Is the bird eating too much greenfood such as lettuce? With a bit of luck, changing the diet leads to an immediate improvement. If this doesn't happen, seek expert advice. Again, diarrhoea is often a symptom rather than an actual illness.

Egg binding see Breeding

Eyes   A discharge coming from the eye(s) is normally treated with a specially-prescribed antibiotic ointment used as directed by the vet.

Feathers (see also Mites) A single budgerigar may feather pluck. Are you giving the bird enough attention? Is it bored? The bird should have

- a more interesting lifestyle
- more attention paid to it
- toys such as a mirror, a bell and a ladder
- the position of the cage changed
- a mate

Some cocks (especially Zebra Finches) feather pluck their mates until they are virtually bald in order to obtain soft nesting material. Did you provide an alternative in sufficient quantities?

When the brood is independent, separate the hen from the other birds. Don't give them a chance to peck and persecute her. To help feather growth, add a few drops of a tonic rich in iron to her drinking water each day.

Take professional advice for other feather disorders, such as loss of primary flight feathers or really tatty, weak-looking plumage.

Limbs Setting and putting a splint on a broken limb is a major problem with a small bird. If your bird has broken its leg or wing:

Did you know?
The mite is a member of the Arachnid family, which also includes spiders, scorpions and ticks.

- remove perches
- put a deep layer of soft hay or moss in the bottom of the cage
- place pots for food and water in the bottom of the cage

Next, ring your vet, say what you have done and get his opinion. A broken wing needs immediate professional examination. The vet will probably set and tape an injured wing.

Mites Your bird should not get mites if you keep its cage clean. The mite *Chemidoctuptes pilae* is the one you are most likely to encounter. It causes scaly beak, scaly face and scaly leg. The encrustation betraying its presence is most likely to be found on the cere of the budgie.

Did you know?
Wild birds have been seen picking up and smearing their plumage with ants. It is thought they are using the formic acid secreted by ants to get rid of mites.

The infection is easily cured with an ointment from your local pet shop. An affected bird will probably rub its beak on a perch to alleviate the irritation, so keep the perches clean until the outbreak has been eradicated. If untreated, scaly beak can lead to distorted or unusual beak growth.

Feather mite symptoms include feather plucking or the constant cleaning of plumage as if the bird had an irritation. You can buy a powder or spray from your pet shop. After you have treated the bird with this, clean and sterilise the cage.

Scaly beak, face and leg see Mites

Did you know?
A mite was once also a small Flemish copper coin of low value.

To sum up

If you were to hang a bird-keeping motto on the wall, it should be 'Prevention is Better than Cure'. Your chances of avoiding any serious problems are then very good.

Unless the condition and cure are simple, get your bird to the vet as quickly as possible. Until then, make sure it is kept warm and unstressed. Even if you can treat the bird yourself, you should always make sure that it is warm and comfortable.

Chapter 10

Joining a bird club

After a while, you will probably want to extend your interests and activities. Bird keeping is a popular hobby and there are lots of different directions in which you can go. You might have been so captivated by the hobby that you have got more birds and started breeding more seriously. Ever open to a challenge, you could even have begun to think about showing your birds in local bird shows.

If you go to a show, look closely at the birds being exhibited. You will see that most, if not all, of the birds have a ring on one leg. There are two sorts of ring: 'closed' and 'split'.

A closed ring is essential if you are going to show a bird. Usually it is obtained from the appropriate national club before the chick is born. The ring identifies the bird's year of birth to make sure it qualifies for the event in which it has been entered. It is fitted when the chick is a few days old and big enough to be handled without ill-effect. Fitting a closed ring is not difficult, but a bird's leg and toes can easily suffer permanent damage in the hands of an inexperienced person, so you should seek the advice of a bird keeper who has experience in that species. He or she will be happy to guide you through the procedures of obtaining and fitting the ring for that species.

Anyone with a bit of experience and confidence can fit a split ring. Unfortunately this type of ring is not acceptable if you wish to show your birds because it can be fitted to a bird of any age.

Of the two sorts, the plastic split ring is the easier to fit as the metal type requires special pliers to close it. Plastic split rings are normally supplied with the fitting tool and instructions. The tool expands the ring which then can be slid over the leg. When the tool is removed, the ring closes.

Advertisements for split ring suppliers can normally be found in either *Bird keeper* or *Cage & Aviary Birds*.

Closed ring

Local clubs

Probably there are lots of clubs in your area although you might not be aware of them. So how do you find out what is going on?

Most bird clubs want publicity and some have a volunteer publicity officer. The local paper is always looking for news to fill its pages and it is the publicity officer's job to oblige it. Therefore your local paper should be a good source of what is going on in the local bird world. My paper, for instance, includes bird shows in its lists of forthcoming events. It generally follows this up by giving good coverage to the more important shows in a later issue.

Split ring

'Haven't got a local paper,' I can hear some of you saying! All is not lost. You can still visit your reference library where there should be a listing of local societies available. This may be in the form of an alphabetical, card-based index. You may have to search this manually, looking for such things as birds; name of species; the so-and-so town cage bird society, and so on.

If the information is computer-based, you search under 'key' words (for example, name of species). You get the same information but it is much quicker and easier.

If you do decide to join a local club you will find the members friendly and helpful. As a matter of routine, the club may organise a different activity for each meeting, which normally takes place once a month. Some clubs even run their own book lending library.

Cage & Aviary Birds lists many local club meetings each week as well as some of the bigger shows.

National clubs

The biggest show of all is the National Cage & Aviary Birds Exhibition. This is just called The National by bird keepers and is normally held in November or early December each year. There you will see both a wide variety of cage and aviary birds and a fascinating display of goods to buy.

Did you know?

The National regularly attracts over 10,000 entries of birds for exhibiting and judging and 20,000 visitors.

The big clubs, who recruit members on a national basis, confine themselves to one species or type of bird. Most will have stands at The National, but you do not have to wait until then to join: clubs are always keen to recruit new members. Addresses can be found in *Useful addresses.*

The rest of this chapter gives some details about the clubs dealing with the species covered by this book. Normally the clubs offer reduced subscriptions to encourage young people to join.

Did you know?

The word bungalow comes from the Hindi 'bangl', meaning 'belonging to Bengal'. A one-storey house used to be common there.

The National Bengalese Fanciers' Association

The National Bengalese Fanciers' Association (NBFA) was formed in 1954. New members receive a wide-ranging question-and-answer sheet which covers the basic care and breeding of the bird. The Association actively encourages its members to show their birds and gives tips on the sort of bird likely to do well.

Did you know?

The original Crystal Palace was erected in Hyde Park for the Great Exhibition of 1851. After this it was moved to Sydenham where it was destroyed by fire in 1936.

The NBFA publishes two magazines a year to let members know what is going on in the Bengalese world. More importantly, it has area representatives who can help to solve any problems you may have.

The Budgerigar Society

The Budgerigar Society (BS) owes its origins to the club of the same name which was formed in 1925 at Crystal Palace, and has about 6000 members. Many of these are beginners who avail themselves of the good selection of books, videos and even computer programmes available. The Society exists to promote the budgerigar on a world-wide basis.

The Society also runs a Pet Owners' Club which caters for those who feel their level of interest does not justify full membership.

Canary

There is no one club for this bird as there are separate clubs for the various varieties.

The Fife Fancy Canary Club

The club, founded in 1957, was the first one formed to cater for Fife Canary enthusiasts. Each year it awards over 100 'patronages' to local cage bird clubs. A patronage allows a paid-up member of the Fife Fancy Canary Club to compete for rosettes and awards on a local, rather than area or national, basis.

The Club has members all over the country. It also sells various items which have the club's name printed on them, and issues an annual newsletter.

The International Gloster Breeders' Association

The International Gloster Breeders' Association (IGBA) was formed in 1966 and is possibly the largest of all the canary clubs. It encourages young members to show their birds and has special Junior Awards at local shows.

A comprehensive handbook is issued twice a year. The Association rules are in the first edition, details of members all over the world are in the second, and names and addresses of area representatives are in both. Your area representative will be pleased to help you if you have any problems.

Similar arrangements apply to overseas countries where the number of members justifies it.

The Zebra Finch Society

The Zebra Finch Society was founded in 1952 and issues three newsletters a year plus an annual year book. More importantly, there is a special Beginner Starter Pack issued to new members for the first two years of membership. A good selection of books and other items is available for members to buy. There are also four regional clubs. The Society has members all over the country which means that if you encounter any difficulties, there is a good chance that the Society can put you in touch with someone near you.

Useful addresses

Magazines

Bird keeper is the leading colour monthly bird-keeping magazine in the United Kingdom and is available from most newsagents. It deals with all breeds of birds and contains both regular and feature articles which reflect the wide variety of birds kept in aviculture. The magazine has subscribers all over the world.

A typical issue could contain articles on the birds covered by this book (budgerigars, canaries and Foreign Finches); lots of other species; practical hints and tips. There is also a directory of avian vets, national clubs and societies plus a Bird Swap Shop & Wanted Service.

Bird keeper
King's Reach Tower
Stamford Street
London SE1 9LS
United Kingdom

Subscription Enquiries: 01444 445553

Cage & Aviary Birds is the leading weekly magazine for bird keepers and is available from most newsagents. It is read by amateurs, experts, breeders and exhibitors all over the world. Like its sister magazine, *Bird keeper*, it has regular articles on an impressively wide range of birds. The magazine also runs a Junior Bird League with its own regular column. Also included are details of local club meetings and shows, plus lots of 'bird for sale' and 'wanted' advertisements.

Cage & Aviary Birds
King's Reach Tower
Stamford Street
London SE1 9LS
United Kingdom

Subscription Enquiries: 0171 261 5000

National clubs and societies

All enquiries to the clubs and associations below should be accompanied by a stamped addressed envelope and addressed to the Hon. Secretary.

National Bengalese Fanciers' Association
2 Bridge Street
Griffithstown
Gwent NP4 5JB
United Kingdom

The Budgerigar Society
49–53 Hazelwood Road
Northampton NN1 1LG
United Kingdom

International Gloster Breeders' Association
5 Halton Drive
Timperley
Altrincham
Cheshire WA15 6AU
United Kingdom

The Zebra Finch Society
309 North Road
Darlington
Co. Durham DL1 2JR
United Kingdom

The Fife canary. You can read about this bird on page 14.

My bird notes

Glossary of terms

Bird keeping, like any other hobby, has its own language which can be confusing for a beginner. Don't worry, you are in good company. Even experienced birdkeepers often have to learn new words if they start to keep a new species.

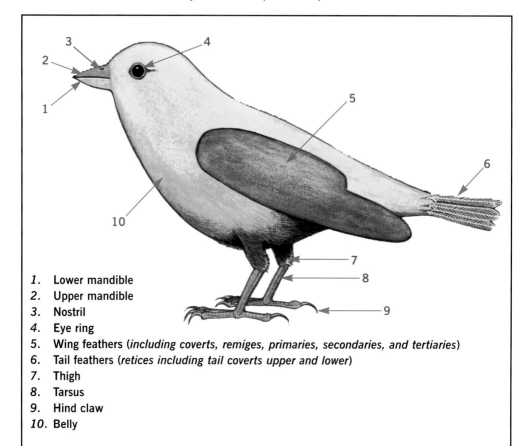

1. Lower mandible
2. Upper mandible
3. Nostril
4. Eye ring
5. Wing feathers (*including coverts, remiges, primaries, secondaries, and tertiaries*)
6. Tail feathers (*retices including tail coverts upper and lower*)
7. Thigh
8. Tarsus
9. Hind claw
10. Belly

This chapter lists some of the terms most commonly used in the bird world.

Addled A fertile egg in which the embryo has died.

Albino A bird which lacks dark pigments in its feathers and eyes.

Aviary A structure normally used to keep birds outside. It consists of a shelter or birdroom attached to a wire flight.

Aviculture The keeping and breeding of birds in cages or aviaries.

Bird bits Magazine articles often contain references to parts of a bird. The most common of these are shown in the diagram on page 56.

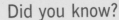

Did you know?
The weight of one clutch of eggs laid by the hen of some finch species can exceed the weight of the hen herself.

Buff Canary feathers which are edged with white.

Cap The top of a bird's head. Mostly used for the gold and silver caps of Lizard canaries.

Cere The bare patch above the beak of a bird.

Chromosome A small, compact-bodied structure which carries an animal's genes.

Clear Either an infertile egg or a bird with only light-coloured feathers.

Clutch The number of eggs laid by a bird before incubation starts.

Cobby A short, thick-bodied bird.

Colour food A special food used to enhance and improve the natural colour of a bird. It is normally fed to canaries.

Consort
The fringeless mate in a pair of birds, one of which is fringed (Corona) and the other unfringed (Consort).

Conspecific Birds which are of the same species.

Corona see Consort.

Crestbred The unfringed offspring of a Consort and Corona.

Did you know?
The crop of a pigeon can contain 500 grains of seed.

Crop The part of the digestive tract of a bird which lies between the oesophagus and stomach. It provides the first stage of the digestive process. It allows a bird to eat a lot of seed quickly, thus reducing the time it is exposed to enemies.

Cross-bred The outcome of the mating of two different species of an animal.

Dead In Shell (DIS) A chick which, unable to break out of its shell, has died.

Dilute A paler plumage colour than you would normally expect to find in that variety of bird.

Display A behavioural pattern used by a bird to attract and secure a mate.

Domesticated A species bred in captivity for generations. Stocks are therefore independent of the wild.

Dominant A characteristic, carried by a gene, which prevails over other genes carrying a similar message.

Fancy Used to describe certain type breeds, such as The Canary Fancy.

Flight feathers The long feathers on a bird's wing.

Fledged A young bird which can fly.

Fledgling A chick still dependent on its parents although it has left the nest.

Flighted A cage and aviary bird which is at least a year old and has moulted for the first time.

Frugivore A bird that eats mainly fruit.

Genes The inherited material, found in the chromosome, carrying the main characteristics of an animal.

Genetic make up The inheritable characteristics of a species.

Gregarious Describes animals which like to gather in a flock.

Hardbill A bird whose diet is principally seed which it cracks open.

Host-specific A parasite which has only one host, or a bird which lays its eggs in the nest of only one other species.

Hybrid The resulting offspring from the mating of two different species (see also Mule).

Inbreeding The mating of closely-related animals.

Insectivore A bird whose diet consists principally of insects.

Lethal gene A gene, possession of which by a parent is fatal to its offspring.

Mealy see Buff.

Melanism/Melanistic Darkness of colour. Caused by unusually excessive development of black pigmentation.

Mule The offspring of a canary mated with another species, often a greenfinch.

Mutation A genetic change producing a noticeable difference in a species.

Nectivore A bird whose diet consists principally of nectar.

Nest feathers The first feathers grown by a chick.

> ### Did you know?
> The female cuckoo lays her eggs only in the nest of the species which raised her.

Normal A cage and aviary bird identical to the wild type.

Oesophagus The tube via which food travels from the mouth to the stomach.

Omnivore An animal with a wide-ranging diet.

Pied A bird with contrasting, broken colouring of light and dark areas.

Plainhead A bird (normally a canary) without a crest.

Preening The grooming process of a bird.

Psittacine A parrot or parrot-like bird, such as the budgie.

Recessive A gene characteristic hidden by the dominant gene.

Roost A place where birds gather to sleep for the night (noun). To settle down on a perch for a night's sleep (verb).

Saddle The middle of the back of a bird.

Self-coloured A bird of just one colour.

Sex-linked Recessive characteristics passed from mother to son.

Softbill A bird whose diet is principally softfood (plants and insects) rather than seed.

Ticked A dark bird with a small light mark on the plumage or a light bird with a dark one.

Tour(s) The song 'book' of a canary.

Type The appearance of a species or variety of a bird required for exhibitions and shows.

Unflighted A bird, less than a year old, which has not yet moulted its nest feathers.

Wild type The wild form of a cage and aviary bird.

Further reading

Budgerigars: your easy guide to training
Paula Jones and Philippa Bower

If you are interested in training your young budgerigar to sit on your hand, fly freely around the room and to speak, then this is the book for you. Drawing on their experience with the talented Rainbow, the authors have written a delightful book to help with all the above. Humourously illustrated, the book will appeal to everyone who has tried or wants to try to give their budgie the best life possible.

ISBN 1 85279026-1

Popular British Birds in Aviculture
Peter Lander and Robert Partridge

For the serious aviculturist, this series of four books provides a wealth of information on the history, care and breeding of British finches. Detailed chapters on genetics will help the breeder to achieve the desired results. Written by two of the most experienced people in the bird world, and generously illustrated with full colour photographs, the books will be required reading for the enthusiast.

Book 1 Greenfinches ISBN 1 85279029 6
Book 2 Siskins and Goldfinches ISBN 1 85279030 X
Book 3 Redpolls, Twites and Linnets ISBN 1 85279031 8
Book 4 Bullfinches, Chaffinches and Bramblings ISBN 1 85279032 6

Bourke's Parakeet
Doreen Haggard

For the first time, a book is available which concentrates solely on this delightful parakeet. It is comprehensive in its coverage of the bird, its origins, care, habits, breeding activity, nutrition, health and colour variations. Full-colour photographs throughout illustrate the myriad activities of this bird, making the book most attractive to read and own.

ISBN 1 85279061 X

All the above books, and more, are available from
TFH/Kingdom Books, PO Box 15, Waterlooville PO7 6BQ, UK

Index